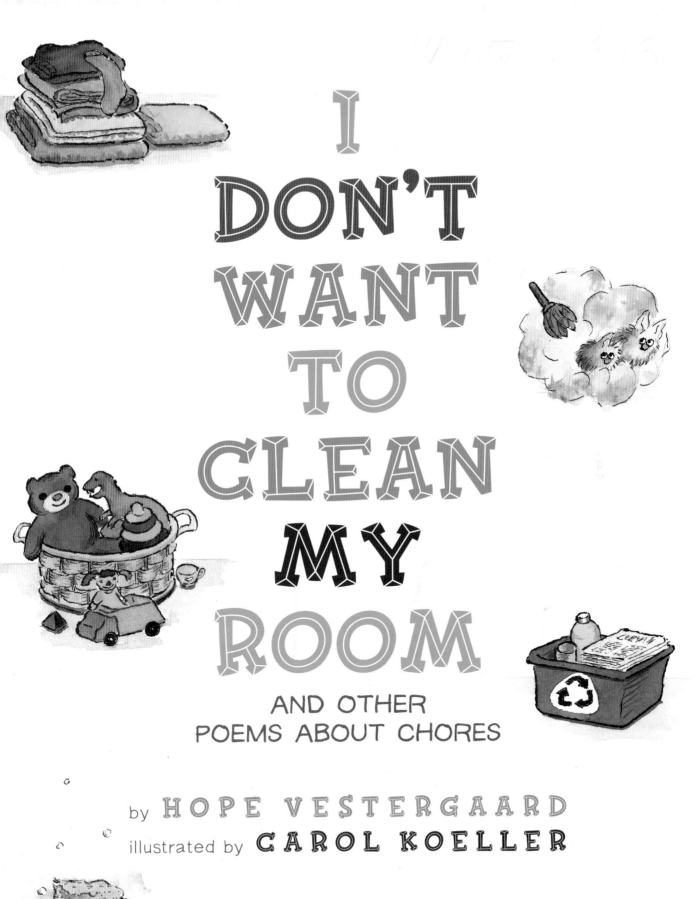

I DON'T WANT TO CLEAN MY ROOM

AND OTHER POEMS ABOUT CHORES

by HOPE VESTERGAARD

illustrated by CAROL KOELLER

DUTTON CHILDREN'S BOOKS

DUTTON CHILDREN'S BOOKS
A division of Penguin Young Readers Group

Published by the Penguin Group • Penguin Group (USA) Inc., 375 Hudson Street,
New York, New York 10014, U.S.A. • Penguin Group (Canada), 90 Eglinton Avenue East,
Suite 700, Toronto, Ontario, Canada M4P 2Y3 (a division of Pearson Penguin Canada
Inc.) • Penguin Books Ltd, 80 Strand, London WC2R 0RL, England • Penguin Ireland,
25 St Stephen's Green, Dublin 2, Ireland (a division of Penguin Books Ltd) • Penguin
Group (Australia), 250 Camberwell Road, Camberwell, Victoria 3124, Australia
(a division of Pearson Australia Group Pty Ltd) • Penguin Books India Pvt Ltd, 11
Community Centre, Panchsheel Park, New Delhi - 110 017, India • Penguin Group (NZ),
Cnr Airborne and Rosedale Roads, Albany, Auckland 1310, New Zealand (a division of
Pearson New Zealand Ltd) • Penguin Books (South Africa) (Pty) Ltd, 24 Sturdee Avenue,
Rosebank, Johannesburg 2196, South Africa • Penguin Books Ltd, Registered Offices:
80 Strand, London WC2R 0RL, England

CIP Data is available.

Published in the United States by Dutton Children's Books,
a division of Penguin Young Readers Group
345 Hudson Street, New York, New York 10014
www.penguin.com/youngreaders

Designed by Irene Vandervoort

Manufactured in China   First Edition
ISBN 978-0-525-47776-1

10 9 8 7 6 5 4 3 2 1

For Stephanie and Sarah, who were a big help!
—H.V.

To my husband, David, and to my wonderful
daughters, Krista and Laura, who, lilke me, don't
always want to clean their rooms.   —C.K.

Bores

It's Saturday,
but I can't play.
I've got chores to do:
wipe the chairs,
sweep the stairs,
find my missing shoe.

I don't *want* to clean my room!
It looks fine to me.
I like my toys out on the floor—
they're easier to see.

Gee!

Can't you get me started?
Show me what to do….
If you help with my jobs,
later, I'll help you.

Bed Head

Shake, shake, shake
the wrinkled sheets,
pull them till they're flat.

Pat, pat, pat.
What's that lump?
Hey! I found the cat!

Fluff, fluff, fluff
the pillows plump.
This part's lots of fun!

Tuck, tuck, tuck
the blankets in.
Phew—I'm nearly done!

Hop, hop, hop!
I'm superkid!
I'll stop in just a minute!

Flop, flop, flop.
This bed looks
kinda comfy with you in it.

Hip, hip, hooray!
Now I can play!
Just let me fix this pile.

Making beds
is so much work,
I need to rest a while.

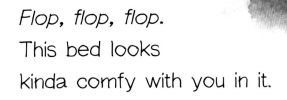

Laundry Day

THIS little baby does not care for toys,
not *even* the ones that have lights and make noise.
There's only one pastime this small girl enjoys—
and THAT is doing the laundry!

The towels! The T-shirts! Pajamas and pants!
She tears through the piles when she sees her chance....
Socks soar through the air as she does her wash dance.
She's singing a song about laundry!

The water is sudsy—now toss in the clothes!
The washer starts shaking and *CHUGS* as it goes.
She peeks at the action from her tippy-toes.
She's keeping her eye on that laundry!

Wee-Cycling

Who can find the tin cans?
   I can, I can!

Who can stomp the milk jugs?
   I can, too!

Can you sort the boxes? Stack the papers?
I can take them to the curb—

with you!

Waiting Tables

While you wait for suppertime,
here's what you can do:
Line the forks up, end-to-end.
Line the plates up, too.

Set out special glasses.
Fold each napkin twice.
Taste the butter, break the bread.
Fill each glass with ice.

Smooth the lumpy tablecloth.
Fill up Mommy's vase.
The only job that's left to do:
Decide which one's your place!

Wishes

Please don't make me stack the dishes.
I don't like to scrape my plate.
Do I *have to* wipe the table?!
Those are all the jobs I hate.

But, OH! I want to fill the sink up!
Can I wear the rubber gloves?
Let me! let me! squeeze the soap in!
These are all the jobs I love.

Bubble Blast

good clean fun!

Handy

When it comes to crumbs,
I'm all thumbs,
so I need a tool.
I've got my own small vacuum—
vrrrooomm. . . .
I think it's pretty cool.

It gobbles up my breakfast.
It tickles on my toes.
It finds the quarters in the couch
and sucks them up its nose.

It's faster than my brother
and louder than the phone.
I love to vacuum all day long. . . .

That's why I'm all alone.

Dust Buster

Whether
I use feathers,
a rag,
or a mop...
once I get to dusting,
it's pretty hard to stop.

I *plink* on the piano,
brush off favorite books,
rearrange the knickknacks,
hide in cozy nooks.

I chase down dusty bunnies
and try on Grandma's lace.
There's only one spot left to clean:
my own dirty face.

Laundry Day II

The spinning has stopped. The washer is done.
Now into the dryer clothes FLY, one by one!
Who cares about playing when work is this fun?
WHOOPEE! She loves doing laundry!

So fluffy and toasty and soft on her skin!
Dad fills up the basket and baby climbs in.
She's wearing her ear-to-ear washing-day grin.
JUST LOOK! She is chin-deep in laundry!

When everything's folded, it's time to relax
among the clean clothing all sorted in stacks.
Now there's only one thing this little girl lacks,
and that's…

MORE DIRTY LAUNDRY!

The Goal

When it's time to clean the floor,
here's a little trick:
A yogurt lid's a perfect puck;
my mop's a hockey stick!

We face off by the oven.
Mom skates around the rink.
I check her with my elbow—
the puck lands in the sink!

Play by play, we clean the floor.
We slosh and slide and scrub.
When Mom forgets to guard her door,
I shoot again...

and SCORE!

Snow Business

Shoveling the snow is tough
when there's so much other stuff
to do with snow:
Like build and throw
and watch your footprints as you go.
Serve your mom an icy treat,
bury both your daddy's feet.
Dig for treasure,
catch a lift,
ride your shovel down the drift!
Shoveling the *walk* is hard...
I prefer to clear the yard.

Paint Complaint

We're giving the fence
a coat of paint—
rail, by rail, by rail.

My bucket of white
is sloshing so,
it leaves a splashy trail.

There's more on us
than on the wood—
or even in my pail.

My arms are tired.
My back hurts, too.
This chore is getting stale. . . .

But—inch by inch,
the fence grows bright—
rail, by rail, by rail.

In the Garden

When summer sun begins to climb,
I find my tools—it's garden time!
We grab our shovels,
hats, and hose,
and get to work between the rows.

Can I water?
Look for weeds.
If we don't, they'll spread their seeds.

Can I water?
First, we hoe.
Turn the soil as you go.

Can I water?
Now we pick.
Look, there goes a walking stick!

Carrots, sweet peas, baby squash...
Don't taste yet—we need to wash.

Can I do it?!
Yes, you may.
Just be careful where you spray...
HEY!

On the Line

It's summertime,
the weather's fine,
and we dry laundry on the line.
I find the socks among the clothes,
and m-a-r-c-h them
down the line
in rows.

Grandma hangs the great big sheets.
They build my walls—
so fresh and sweet!
I stay there,
quiet as a mouse,
and play inside my laundry house.

Hot Dog

It's my turn to wash the dog!
He's getting kind of smelly.
There's something sticky on his tail—
I think he wagged in jelly.

He sees the hose.
He tries to run!
But I hold on real tight.
When we're done,
my sister laughs…
he's clean, but we're a sight!

All Done

The wood is stacked.
The leaves are raked.
My toys are picked up, too.
The trash is tucked inside the can—
just see what **we** can do!

The tub is scrubbed,
the windows washed.
The house smells sweet and new.
And everything looks twice as nice
because I cleaned with **you**.